spot

BACKYARD ANIMALS

ROBINS

by Mari Schuh

AMICUS | AMICUS INK

chest

nest

Look for these words and pictures as you read.

eggs

beak

A robin chirps
in the trees.

Robins are songbirds.
Their calls are like songs.

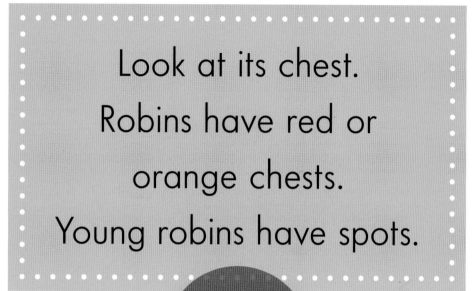

Look at its chest.
Robins have red or
orange chests.
Young robins have spots.

chest

Look at the nest.
It is shaped like a bowl.
It is made of twigs,
mud, and grass.

nest

Look at the eggs.
Each egg is the size
of a quarter.
They will hatch
in two weeks.

eggs

beak

Look at the beak.
It grabs berries. Yum!

A robin pokes its beak into the soil. It pulls out a worm! Time to eat!

chest

nest

Did you find?

eggs

beak

spot

Spot is published by Amicus and Amicus Ink
P.O. Box 1329, Mankato, MN 56002
www.amicuspublishing.us

Library of Congress Cataloging-in-Publication Data
Names: Schuh, Mari C., 1975- author.
Title: Robins / by Mari Schuh.
Description: Mankato, MN : Amicus/Amicus Ink, [2019] |
   Series: Spot. Backyard animals | Audience: K to grade 3.
Identifiers: LCCN 2017052463 (print) | LCCN 2017055187
   (ebook) | ISBN 9781681515854 (pdf) | ISBN
   9781681515472 (library binding) | ISBN 9781681523859
   (pbk.)
Subjects: LCSH: American robin–Juvenile literature. | Rob-
   ins–Juvenile literature.
Classification: LCC QL696.P288 (ebook) | LCC QL696.P288
   S38 2019 (print) | DDC 598.8/42–dc23
LC record available at https://lccn.loc.gov/2017052463

Printed in China

HC 10 9 8 7 6 5 4 3 2 1
PB 10 9 8 7 6 5 4 3 2 1

Mary Ellen Klukow, editor
Deb Miner, series designer
Kazuko Collins, book designer
Holly Young, photo researcher

Photos by Alamy 4–5, 6–7, 12–13; Getty
10–11; iStock cover, 1, 3, 8–9, 14

ROBINS